This Changing Earth

Harcourt
SCHOOL PUBLISHERS

Orlando   Austin   New York   San Diego   Toronto   London

Visit *The Learning Site!*
www.harcourtschool.com

Earth Changes

What makes up the surface of Earth? You can look for clues. You might see sand or stones on the ground. Near beaches or mountains you might see large rocks or cliffs.

Earth is made up of rock. The rock near the surface of Earth is called the crust. It is cool. The rock below Earth's crust is a lot warmer.

Rocks near the shore are a clue. They help tell us what Earth is made of.

You might think rock is so hard that it never changes. But Earth's crust changes all the time. Some things like wind and water make rock change very slowly. Other things can make rock change very quickly.

 CAUSE AND EFFECT What are two things that cause changes to Earth's crust?

Some changes to the surface of Earth take many years.

Slow Surface Changes

Rock can be worn away slowly over time. **Weathering** happens when wind and water break down rock into smaller pieces.

Wind carries grains of sand, which are tiny pieces of broken rock. They act like sandpaper to wear down large rocks. Water in rivers tumbles rocks and breaks them. Water freezes in the cracks of rocks. The ice forces the cracks apart until the rock breaks.

Frozen water takes up more space than liquid water. It causes the ground to crack. It even breaks rocks.

The Grand Canyon is the result of weathering and erosion by a river.

Weathering breaks down rock. Where do all the tiny pieces go? Wind and water carry them to new places. This is called **erosion**. A flowing river can carry away small rock pieces. It drops them in new places where the river slows down.

CAUSE AND EFFECT
What two effects do wind and water have on rock?

Fast Fact

The Grand Canyon was formed by erosion. Some scientists think it took five to six million years to form.

Changes Inside Earth

The surface of Earth is a rocky crust. Inside Earth is a warm center. The center is made of hot, melted rock. The hard crust is always moving over the hot center. This can make big changes happen fast on the surface.

During an earthquake, the ground can break apart.

An **earthquake** is a shaking of Earth's surface. This happens when the rock crust moves suddenly. An earthquake can push Earth's surface up. This makes mountains. An earthquake can also push the surface down. This can make lakes.

When an earthquake happens under water, it causes huge waves.

 CAUSE AND EFFECT What causes earthquakes?

Earth's surface can rise or fall when an earthquake happens.

More Fast Changes

Volcanoes cause other fast changes on Earth. A **volcano** is a place in Earth's surface where hot melted rock flows to the surface. This hot rock is called lava. The lava hardens as it cools.

Fast Fact

Lava from a volcano can be hotter than 750 degrees Celsius (1,382 degrees Fahrenheit).

Hot rock may soon flow from this volcano as lava.

Hot, melted rock from a volcano changes the surface of the land around it.

Hot lava burns the trees and plants around the volcano. As the hot rock cools, it forms a layer of rock. Mountains are formed as this happens over and over. In time, new trees and plants grow.

COMPARE AND CONTRAST How does a volcano change the surface of Earth?

Exploring Changes

There are many kinds of landforms on the surface of Earth. Some are tall. Some are flat. There are high mountains and flat deserts. There are islands, and there are deltas.

You know that earthquakes and volcanoes can form mountains. Did you know that volcanoes can form islands?

Many islands are formed by underwater volcanoes.

Small rocks and dirt carried by the river formed this delta.

Erosion can form a delta. A delta is land that forms where a river meets a large body of water. The river drops sand and soil there.

 COMPARE AND CONTRAST How is a delta different from an island?

Summary

Earth is made up of rock. Weathering and erosion slowly change Earth's surface. Earth's surface can also change quickly. Earthquakes and volcanoes cause fast changes.

Glossary

earthquake A shaking of Earth's surface that can cause land to rise or fall (7, 10, 11)

erosion Change caused when wind and water move sand and small rocks to a new place (5, 10, 11)

volcano A place where hot melted rock called lava comes out of the ground onto Earth's surface (8, 9, 10, 11)

weathering Change caused when wind and water break down rock into smaller pieces (4, 5, 11)